Dixi in His Cups

Richard "Dixi" Cohn

Dixi in His Cups

poems by Richard "Dixi" Cohn

Malthus Press

Malthus Press
2317 B Carleton Street
Berkeley, California 94704-3316

ISBN 1-883456-08-8

The cover illustration is based on a photograph of Dixi by
Louis Cuneo .

Cover by Marcia Poole.

Cover Illustration copyright 2003 by Marcia Poole.

"Oedipus Pete" illustration by Mike La Bash.

This book is produced exactly as Dixi requested.

Printed in U.S.A.

to all of the many friends, family and poets, doctors and nurses, social workers, administrative workers, financial counselors who are helping me in this struggle of my life, not to forget my fellow employees and bosses at Discount Cameras, everyone at U.S. Social Security, Herrick-Alta Bates Cancer Clinic and Hospital, Pacific Hematology & Oncology in Fountain Valley, California, Southwest Airlines, Air Angel Network, The American Cancer Society, The Harvey Family,
Like an old Jazz song goes,
"I thought about you",
And like the "Duke" used to say,
"I love you all madly".

– Richard N. "Dixi" Cohn

Contents

Introduction

"GooOOOD EveNing, Sports Fans!" Big toothful grin a
Bronx mile wide. "That's my usual greeting," Dixi smiles out
from under his beret, snuggled deep into his SF Giants jacket,
holding a big wad of poems in his fist. He's prepared to read
tonight. Folks in their chairs recross their legs, refold their
arms, get ready for the barnstormin' moment that's about to
unfold.

Dixi sways, his voice ranging from whisper to wail to
the ricochet rhythm of the cityscape, the busways, up from
the classical, through every imaginable occupation to keep
things square with the village and keep up the vendor patter
normally experienced at a baseball game, because the
underlying camera, eye touching into images onto paper,
moving, ever moving like the heart that beats the daily
squalor of urban beauty through veins of triumph, Dixi sings,
the room is still, Buddha is resting at everyone's table at once,
an explosion of laughter, even the air has become riveted to
the vibration viscerally climbing the scale of intention, Dixi
waves his arms, the slug of papers in his hand rattle against
the shadows, Dixi romps, roars, and slaps the face of every
consciousness within earshot...

Then everybody realizes it's time for applause. Yes,
let the applause begin, for the work herein presented, where
it's easy to recognize that Dixi's poems (and sometimes
prose) give proof of the pudding: there's a real reason when
you choose a word to use in the universe.

– Randy Fingland

Dalai Lama Phone Call

Ring, Ring, Ring, Arama
if you got a call from
the Dalai Lama,
would you travel to AlaBama,
discourse the story of your life,
a Dram-a-Rama,
Don't forget to bring
your Pan-A-Rama Cam-ra,
Perhaps the Lama
Would Dally-a-dama?
Would he sing,
Lama, Dama, ding, dong?,
a-Zama,
tell you bout Tibet,
Opp-ress-a-Whamma,
Fab-U-loso A-Rama,
Lama, Dama, ding, dong,
Tinkle, A-Lama.

— July 16, 1993

1

Reprinted from Cherotic Revolutionary #3!

"Oedipus Pete"

Note: The nickname given to the unfortunate ballplayer by Lowell Cohn (no relation), columnist for the *San Francisco Chronicle*, in a very literate sports piece comparing him to Oedipus of Greek fable who was forced to leave his Greek city for unbecoming conduct.

"Oedipus Pete" was fleet on his feet,
    ran the bases like no one can,
    had more hits than Ty Cobb,
    many bases did rob,
    made his fans' hearts...throb,
    so they nicknamed him "Charlie Hustle".

Over others, Rose he in the game,
    gaining a name, in the sport of great fame
    known as Baseball,
    the national religion played out in the fall,
    Pete its high priest, the player with gall,
    Oedie Pete, really played ball,
    and often played the World Series...delirious.

But Pete's secret life,
    known perhaps...to his wife,
    but especially...his Bookie,
    who knew Pete bet Red,
    and contracted him dead
    for not paying on time
    to cover his bets made on Baseball.

Yeah! Pete had the life,
  a cute lovin wife,
  and on the side, sly nookie.
His failure was thus,
  feet of clay he did bust
  forfeiting loans from his Bookie.
He'd had money and fame, Rose to the top of the game,
  one day heard his name, for the Hall of Fame,
  called over prairie and plain,

But the media doth say,
  Oedipus Pete bet on Baseball!
  Denial! sayeth he,
  but Giamatti say Yay,
  still Pete exclaimeth, Nay,
  bet on Baseball?...<u>NO WAY</u>!!

But the thing Pete forgot,
  when religion ya got (and Baseball's the national religion),
  don't spill blood on its altar.
  Topple idols of Ball,
  you'll lie and you'll stall,
  throw your career...over the wall!
  But most of all,
  Pete...LOOK!!,
  if you jes paid off the Book,
      Pete!!

Your life would be all quiet and neat,
  but you risked it all for a buck,
  and now, all we can say is,
      Oy! What a Schmuck!

Snap-Shot

Transported again through the Trans-Bay Terminal,
an afterwork extravaganza, rushing to and fro,
back and forth, pell mell, city to city,
looping the Bay Bridge, each day, six days a week,
a fifteen minute ride home this Saturday night,
not soon enough for a twenty-four hour respite,
until the Molochian cycle begins again,
the daily descent into the belly of the beast,
Monday running the camera shop treadmill,
pushing thirty-five millimeter cameras over hot counters,
in a fluorescently lit graveyard of a photo shop ubiquitously,
called Wood Lawn (or, for you West Coasters, Forest Lawn)
with lights, or the S.Y., "Saffa-teria",
selling words, air promises, toothpicks, napkins, salt, ketchup,
water, a cheap meal ticket, wrapped in an Oriental plastic,
bucket of ad copy, high tech jargon, bullshit dream machine,
that essentially haven't changed since George Eastman blew
out his brains, pushed a button, while someone else did the
rest, and developed his ideas into a Mephistophlian machine,
mundane, bundle of switches, printed circuits, relays, time
displays, computerized, homogenized, pasteurized, plastic
and paper, plasticized, manurized, so-called pieces of glass
elements, envisioned ancient Dinosaurs of wooden boxes,
brassed metallic, machines of the eighteenth and nineteenth
centuries, pistoning, a leap forward to our new, new, all new,
automated, autofocusing, pieces of dreck, now merchandized
by the likes of: Minolta, Canon, Nikon, Pentax, Vivitar,
Konisheroko, Leitz, Yashica and Zeiss. We've had
masterpieces from the likes of: Niepsche, Herschel, Saloman,
Latique, Bresson, Brassi, Adams, Doisneau, Bravo, Capa,
Weston, Steiglitz, Steichen, Lange, Bourke-White, Meisel,
Meiselas, Eisenstein, Arbus, Steiner, Haas, Smith, Uzzle,

Camponigro, Cameron and countless others omitted by
faulty memory and spacial limitations, something magical
fabricating and capturing the light from darkness, laundering
preparations from the bones of long-dead animals, emulsified
and blended with precious metallic, silvered, T-grained cells
locked like Lot's wife, salted into gelatin, reprojected,
reformed. Blasting these graven images electronically, around
the world, in seconds. Beamed by satellite even to the
farthest reaches of outer space. While the Kodak, Orwo,
Fuji, Agfa, Ilford, Russian and Chinese factories spool it en
masse by blind people, for more the two hundred years when
Brady left us a legacy of still born instant slices of U.S. Grant,
time machined, Leica'd, images, polarized moving images in
succession, blurring, a kaleidoscope in motion to a standing
still Polaroid, as we are, standing still dumfounded. And the
great universal mystery turns, steadily on its own axis,
"Tempus, tempus fugit", time does not stand still for anyone
-- or thing like it or not, our span of being here is marked
and finite, a jot or second in the, vast, flowing, infinite ocean
of time.

And who shall remember us? Who will light a
YarZeit candle and recite the Kaddish when we become the
crushed recycled bones of the world, wormed, becoming
flashes of light, of the process. Becoming faded recording on
plastic, magnetic tape or floppies, graven images in color or
black and white, some lost in floods, earthquakes, fires of
mirrored lives, that are no more, other beings, our ancestors,
anaoymous strangers. Aliens yet to reinhabit this or other
planets. Will they ask, Who were these people? Of lost
worlds, combining with the great unconscious spirit.

Will the lab lose your precious film, negatives, the
salacious stuff that made the blood rush from your brain
through the cerebral cortex to your genitals? The wedding or
divorce done or undone. Your dog Charlotte run over, you

grieved for weeks, the freeze-dried look and smell of it all, relatives, Mother, Father, Brother, Sister, forgotten Aunts, Uncles, Cousins, Lovers, real or unreal, make believe, lost gone to the wars of Vietnam, Korea, World Wars One and Two, gone, gone, down on the <u>Un</u>-Sinkable TiTanic, burned up in the <u>Ex</u>-ploded Hindenburg. Smashed in the fall of so many aircraft, gone up in the smoke of the "Death Camps", All this . . . . All this . . . . But for this faded thing, called simply . . . . a photograph.

— *Written to "Rondo a la Turk" by Dave Brubeck*

— 1993

Crapshoot

Do not think that I don't know that I am not condemned,
       I am gambling everything,
The sentence plays out silently, almost undetectable,
       except revealed by the C-Scan;
My Physician tries to rush the telling Me of the readings,
       but I force the issue, understanding His reluctance,
That I might anguish about that knowledge,
       that ravages my body from within;
We're anxious to begin the new compassionate chemo
regime,
       of promise, perhaps?
But I know I'm back in the big casino again,
       where the house can load the dice and stack the deck;
It's a crapshoot for a miracle,
       as I prepare to fly south for the compound.;
It's liquid seep into my veins for some kind of remission,
       and hope it doesn't screw me up too much,
But everyone around Me breathes heavy when I tell them,
       and behind My back they whisper,
GOD, I'm glad it isn't me! or think it,
       tongue wagging about the stricken;
Hell, the condemned can't appreciate everyday's common,
       reality trying not to forget to act normal,
And after the fifteen minute Dr's visit,
       to check me out and my demeanor,
One of my social workers has smoothed the details of travel
for me,
       she is pregnant with new life to birth;
Ironic as my mortality stares me in the face and in my mouth,
       But what can one say or do in this situation?
Say nothing, as the clock ticks, the tumors enlarge,
       insidiously trying to kill me;

I know, I know, but I'll be damned if I just let it happen,
and lose everything like a dumb loser!
So I'll submit to more medical crapshoots,
hoping my number isn't up,
That I still hold some sort of hand, and lady luck is in my fingers,
as I shoot 'em again!
Blow, blow on them for luck.

— March 22, 1998

ButterFly

To my place of employ you did stray,
                                    one long day,
Imploring my help, to copy your artwork,
                                    Now today, please!,
                                    you say,
Now to photograph my work,
                                    to freeze it, to stay,
Should I give it away, now, I fear,
                                    or lose it this day?
I the while struck by your beauty,
                                    in this part,
The loss of creation,
                                    creation thou art,
Duality of Lady, craft, sought,
                                    the enigma of beauty,
Art is your passion,
                                    I thought,
Lo, the connection
                                    of you to your heart,
The beautiful perfection,
                                    via Josephine's art.
Bewitched, think I, you said "Jennifer",
                                    your name instead,
Unremembering, 'twas Josephine
                                    that you said,
Methinking of Donovan's old sixties song,
                                    Jennifer,
                                    rung in my head,
Stay awhile longer,
                                    I thought I said,
But rush away, in disarray,
                                    you did instead.

10

Months later you reappear,
                    to thank my advice that day,
                    you say,
And away you go again,
                    with the give me a call,
And here's my card and number,
                              blithely we do part.
You mumble of your support through your art,
Out the door of the store,
                    into the night,
Like a dream,
          gone again, Josephine,
Tantalized by your dance and your flight,
                              o damn hapstance,
Your flashing, Butterfly prance,
                    large dark eyes,
                         remembering perchance,
Divine enchantress,
               flighty thing,
Hear the God's laugh,
                    my last feeble chance,
Cursed fool, still knows no goodWoman's love,
Always a star crossed,
                    She from above,
It's always Goodbye,
                    Ne'er to stay,
They just up,
          and run away.
I curse,
      and beseech!
But like the rare Butterfly,
               they fly,
                    out of reach.
      – December 1994

For the Nurse with the Radiant Smile

I just keep wondering,
                working in this place,
        where so many of us are fighting for our lives,
the "Pale Horseman" may sweep us at any time to that far
country,
                across the River Styx,
        and reduce our multitude,
                whenever He may choose.
How do you keep that radiant smile and cheerful attitude
            that shields us for awhile from ourselves, and "Him",
                whilst we are in your presence?

                        – September 10, 1997

St. Paddy of the Day

I became an Irish Catholic quite some time ago when I was about this high. My first visit to the O'Keefe household in the North Bronx. Unprepared for his wild three boys and doe-eyed daughter plus devout in-laws and wife, all in a sprawling seven-room apartment groundfloor on St. Lawrence Ave.

       Upon entering the apartment through the kitchen with the Sacred Heart of Jesus' eyes following you off the wall past the full standing holy water pedestal basin, past a long dark ten-foot foyer-corridor walking into an eerily lit room past a full-sized six-foot standing statue of the Mother Mary, another short corridor, right angle, left turn coming across O'Keefe's father-in-law prostrated on the floor mumbling a Latin-laced Mary full of grace incantation before another five-foot Pieta with his wife screaming and sobbing and scaring the BeJESUS out of me running back down the short and then longer corridor back left turn, reverse right turn, right angle, eerily lit candled foyer into the kitchen, slamming into the holy-watered pedestal basin, the Sacred Heart Jesus's eyes on me, splashing the holy watered stuff all over me and the kitchen floor while the O'Keefe kids taunted and chanted, "Ritchie's a Jew Catlick boy, Ritchie's a Catlick nowwwwww!!".

Rite of Passage, Part I: Locomotion

Four-thirty in the morning. For lack of sleep, the mind spewing forth the imagery as my "Muse" dictates, I monklike pushing the stylus about the papyrus slavishly, as the characters emerge from the ink. It is the "Hour of the Wolf" as the sounds of the Southern Pacific freight lumber along their West Berkeley right of way, the steel wheel clickety clack and mournful whistle echoing way up here in North Berkeley's quietude from the vehicular traffic only hours away from dawn's lemming rush hour. These sounds engulfing the territory as it pushes through them, as those steely beasts with different proprietary names have always done regardless of place or time touching something deeply within human existence.

It seems to this correspondent to always have been within earshot of most of my domiciles. Growing up within a cityblock of railtraffic the railroad lifemark of rite of passage. Emphasizing keypoints of a life. These lumbering electrified, diesel or steam beasts of locomotion carrying human commerce and passengers, the locomotion defined by my mini-Oxford succinctly as the ability to move from place to place.

The ever-present screeching embrace of steel to steel turning wheel to rail tight turns of the elevated subway Number 3 Line in the borough of the Bronx. The elevated structure overriding the right of way while lifting one from the dark subterranean tunnels of sepentinian perpetual night bursting forth into brilliant sunshine or the polluted grey or rainy day. Its distinctive sound in motion carrying individuals, lovers, knaves, thieves, messengers, workers, louts, beggars, etc., etc., etcetera. This distinctive hodgepodge accompanying the daily ground-grind of everyday life on dismal streets, penetrating the pathetic dwelling walls of the

14

city's vertical existence. With all manner of grieving lives trying to survive in these little apartmented cells of space, packed together like it or not.

While politicians waged a "Cold War" with the "Commies" reminding us in the dailies and with the everyday sirens of atomic terror to a simplistic "Duck and Cover" terrifying mindlessness of the "Nuclear Society". We had become Packard's "Nation of Sheep" as the ruling class advertised "Truth, Justice, and the American Way" with breakfast and dinner. The ridiculous bluff and shell game keeping us in line.

And a few blocks away running alongside the Bronx River, New York Central freights carried the goods of Capitalistic commerce greased by the wages of lucre of millions of hands. Paid for by blood, sweat and tears of working men and women to bring food to their tables, clothes to hide their nakedness. Raising families of children so that they shall negotiate the terrain of human society, perhaps?

The mournful whistle sounds piercing neighborhoods, consciousnesses. Unchanging subconscious message, something immortal from generation to generation of railroad men, the promise of escaping from a life beset by woe and drudgery or terror. The hobo promise of transport to a new place, new life of encouragement, hope. Abandoning the life of "No Exit". The whistle and the message of come with me, clickety clack, don't look back. Clambering aboard a westbound freight for free being pulled by the machined, oily beast of burden, blowing steam, braking new tight turns on this "Celestial Railroad", right of passage carrying the Kerouacian Dharma Bum life to the new poetry of experience.

– October 21, 1999

Pigeon Caller

Every morning I'm home,
        his high-pitched whistling
awakens me;
at the edge of sleep, just out of dreaming,
        I begin to hear the whistling,
repetitive signaling from pursed lips,
alerting me to his presence, downstairs,
        outside my window;
the ritual begins about nine A.M.;
        the seemingly continuous high-pitched calling
goes on for at least twenty minutes;
from all of South Berkeley's precincts,
        almost a hundred pigeons and doves,
descend on Fairview Street for their morning tidbits,
scattered by the caller.
Others of his ilk in New York or Boston or Chicago,
San Francisco, Hoboken, Brooklyn, The Bronx of my youth,
pigeon callers all echo their distinct signal
to the creatures of the air, fragile, tough, flighty buggers,
respond to the call, return, returning's in the blood,
their genes, the ritual of ancient revolving,
calling these spirits of the air,
        dear departed beings, return, respond,
completing the cycle, the trip home, this enigma of arrivée,
        returning, returning home.

                    — January 31, 1995

16

Mother-Board

Oh Baby!
      I'd love to ply your software,
Make no mistake,
      These words are sexy "Wordperfect",
Your adorable little mouse nibbles at my "Mainframe brain",
      I wanna byte those big apples of yours,
I've got 250K on board,
      And it's a "Mother"!
I'll ram my 6 ½ inch disk in,
      Baby it's a "Hard drive",
Oh darlin, your "Mac" is stacked,
      I'll find your little "Floppy",
Don't worry, my "D" is "Base",
      So "Decoding" your "Program"
Will be a snap!
      I'm a tough old "Billy Gate",
Be sure to leave all your "95" "Windows" open,
      I'll crawl through,
and lick all your "Dip switches" clean!
      I wanna make
All your "Fonts" wet!
      Can't help being an "E-Mail" "Merger",
So don't let me go, "Microsoft"
      And you'll come in "Reams",
"Online" and in "Full color",
      "Bubble jetting" all over me,
Baby with me, you're always "14K".

– 1996

Clinical JaZZ

JaZZ can help to save your life!
Alone in the Cancer clinic receiving my "Hi-Test", chemo,
Suffusing through my tiny Sony FM Walkman into my ears,
The KCSM highway being driven right now by Dick Conte,
     spinning
his educated mix of JaZZ sound, and all I hear now is:
A synchronous melange, a sax, drum, trombone, clarinet,
     trum-pet
Can give one's mind that necessary dis-tract-ion to sur-vive,
a drum's tack, tack...tacky, tack...tack..subtle, brushhh...shhhh,
As I glance to the IV tubing, drop, drop, drop, drops, steady
ca...denccce...drop..drop..drop..ping, slid...ing, into my
     ..veinssss,
I read my tomes of poe..sie, head...phones..in place,
The rich panoply of JaZZZ, surrounds my brain,
Needed dis..trac..tion, the brass tim..bre of
trum..pets and drum, ..trom...bone,
Mod..dern JaZZ....writing a tome, of its own,
While...a..Bass strummms,..theat rhythm, soft..ly brush..ing,
     snare... drum...skin,...brushh...ing, drum,
And the Omni 5, IV, steadily pumps the Hi..Test, through
     ...me,
As a Sax breathe..sss a Ja..ZZy "Ship Go'in to New York",
Joe's stops, breaking like the waves of a JaZZz..riv..er,
Lapping at my sens..ory shore, the jux..ta..posit..ion of those
riffs...cas..cad..ing, off the fing..er..ing, and brea-thing
mouth-piece actin, emit-ting a man'ss feel..ings,
As a flu-gel horn, jumps in pickingup thespeed, stacca-to
     bursts, riff-ing off the Chi, breathing, breath action,
fin-ger-ing, jumping to gui-tar strings, but fing-er-ing,
         cat-gut strings,
The left hand loving struts, along its neck, and alto-gether,

blend as one, catch-ing the fervor of the rhythm,
as they suffuse to the thing I call my JaZZ Muse,
And Dick chan-ges my per-spective, spinning Irene R's
    "What a Difference a Day Makes",
      Oh shades of Din-ah,
Singing just above the back-up,
The human voice instrumen-tally, a kar-ma of its own,
the vocal chords...push-ing air in-to ma-jik,
Lawd what a difference a day makes & the difference is you,
A sax's refinery accom-panies Irene,
punc-tu-ated by the vibr-ato of gui-tar strings,
HOW? CAN YOU NOT LOVE THIS STUFF!
My KCSM DJ's a collective mind of ind-ivid-uals that seem
    to

              play as
              one,
This eclectic mix of, sensi-bilities from where the JaZZ
      flows like a river,
Eddy-ing, pushing over rocks and rolling, rippling into
      the purity that is, Ameri-can JaZZzz,
A pure, true, clean form, that represents us 'round the
      world,
Synapses flashing to the deepest love that JaZZ ex-presses,
A man for a woman, and vice-versa,
and in this modern age, man for man, or lady to each other,
This connection, a feeling for one's roots and place, shared
over drinks, smoking out our heartbreak, punctuated by the
      sounds of JaZZ
With the Blues, some things only that musik can express,
the special timbre of feeling that Miles could play out,
walking 'round the stage looking into his soul to mirror our
    collective feelings as a people regardless of your race,
or the golden standard "Oldies", Ben Webster could ring out
    your heart with, that golden vibrato, so distinctive, like a

trademark,
or The Bird, wailing in the wilderness, to express his pain &
        joy,
                blowing from his gut to posterity.
Those voices still cry out to us, these Jazz poets, wielding
their instruments sometimes like weapons to awaken out soul.
Too many to name here, unfortunately, but you know them
if you love   love JaZZ as I do.

                              — February 23, 1998

DJ
(for Keith Hines)

Something
        bout a hotel room
for me a way station
        this lonely room.
                    But no distraction
        at times
      cept the drumming.
        Man,
don't get me wrong.
             Dad was a Drummer,
But it's an "Ax"
        gets my stuff groovin,
              my mojo workin.
That voodoo,
      Sax an Piano,
             wailin! wailin, the Blues,
that reflection of aloneness,
           call it loneliness,
no someone to share it with,
      Sax & Piano, Guitar & Organ,
        And of course,
        The Drummers.
It's Existential,
          the sound erases the blues away,
Transposes you, send you away,
            "A Blue Highway",
From the gut of a musician,
          talkin through his "Ax",
Oh Man! What only JAZZ can do...

           – April 27, 1998

21

La Belle et Terrible Saison (or The Her-a-caines)

The Her-a-Caines shall roar and tear up your personal
landscape,

Wind in a season of terrible beauty.

They have names like:
            Connie, Martha, Mary, Charlotte, Caroline,

Blowing through your soul,
            Coursing through your veins,
                        The blood of your existence,
Sending your blood pressure higher,
                        The Fahrenheit picks up,
                                    98, 99, 100,
                102 and beyond,
Delirious now,
            Invading the ocean of your being,
                                    Beyond infinity,
                                                It seems,
Your personal "El Niño" is coming,
                        See the warning signs:
Grey clouds are billowing,
                        A storm approaches,
Imagining in your feverish state,
                        You hear "Mishnoons",
                                    Crazy people,
Talking to themselves,
                        Speaking in tongues,
                                    With the spirits
Of air, fire, and water,

                    Suddenly!
A vortex appears,
          Approaching, twisting, spiraling,
                              As if summoned by,
your unconscious,
          And nature's subterranean system,

          One by one
              You recall the her-a-caines,
                              Year by year,

Caroline 67, Connie 80, Mary 90, Charlotte 95, Martha 92,

Passing through your country,
                              Pounding your harbor and seashore,
Raining relentlessly,
              Tearing you up,
                         Your planet whipped to a frenzy,

Remembering sunny days,
                    Even the slightly rainy ones,
                                   Singing in the rain,
Fire, wind, and water take their toll of you.
                    Blowing the emotions, hot and cold,

Finally you see an Angel in the eye of the storm,
                              Pointing the way,
As you crawl through the desert,
              In a very dry season,
              Remembering
When the her-a-caines
              Passed through your life.

                    – March 1997

                    23

For David Lerner

Here I am,
        Four fifty-five A.M.,
                The "Hour of the Wolf",

           Thoughts of you won't let me sleep,
Struggling with yourself,
                fearing the darkside,
That awful place confronting oneself,
                    a primeval thing,
Always with you,
           unable to defend against,
                    alone,

Clinging,
        to a Mother who loved too much,
Disabled,
        by a sick and angry Father,
              imprinting madness,

The familial "Cold War",
           co-existence,
              of the '50's,

Semitic upbringing,
           constipated life,
              to escape from,
Hypocritic Temple rules,
           mouthing convenient dis-allowance,

They never understood the chemical imbalance of your mind,

the juggling act,
that pushed you to the edge of isolation,

Your demons running amuck,
tearing you up,
A token on your tongue
to ease the pain,
A syringe to quench the fire in your brain,
the burning in your heart,

Tough scribbled analysis
brilliant poetic prose,
Deep emotion spoken with a whispered smoky voice
We shall never hear again from your soul,

What pain,
we tried to know,
but couldn't understand,
Stumbling on your coattails,
showing the inferno of your life,
Thought we might understand your pain,
help ease it a little,
But now we're left,
suddenly suspended

in mid-air,

To suffer,
your absence,
forever,

Choking on your mortality.
— July 9, 1997

Crawl in my skin, feel my bones,
Feel my bones, take my skin,
After we finished the old, in and out,
I momentarily satiated, she a bit richer,
Feel my bones,
We sat together and I cried to her of my miseries,
of my cheating wife,
bored and disdainful of my life,
coming home after the daily toiling,
wiped out, on the couch, watching the idiot flickering tube,
Beached Whale, she said mockingly, beached whale,
Not what I expected, she said,
feel my bones, crawl through my skin,
She played, she cheated as I toiled in the selling fields,
In the retail mines, panning pockets for gold,
bones, skin, skin and bones,
doing the old capitalist dance, the shakedown,
Bones, bones, skin,
riding the long commuter trains and buses,
of the killing commute, bones, bones,
to the cornacopedic cities, the labyrinth,
skin, skin, bones,
a suburban mouse scurrying to mount the wheel, the wheel,
for cheese, turning, turning, skin and bones,
a Tempus clock slave, tick tock, bones, skin, bones,
through the years, now alone, just skin and bones,
skin and bones, alone...................

A New Experience

Have Super Sex with SCREAMER!!!
Not a prophylactic,
Not a contraceptive,
Not a French Tickler,
Not for the timid,
use with, or without, a condom.
If she is a Moaner,
this will make her a <u>SCREAMER</u>!!!
If she is a <u>SCREAMER</u>,
This will get you <u>ARRESTED</u>!!!

Make a little go a LONG, LONG way,
a device, designed,
to pro-long males' cli-max
while stim-u-lating her
in just the - right - place.

*(Found poem from ad posted to men's room
wall in Ginsberg's Pub, February 1990)*

27

Blaspheme

Upon a Berkeley sunny morn,
      awoke did I
with thoughts blasphemic in my brain
      of Zaidas, Saints, and Buddhas born
into this world.
      Is it too vain?
Or sacrilegious falderal,
      my elocution, just some corn,

I think not I thought,
      to see them frail and human.

Consider Father Moses
      descending from the Holy Mount.
So many days;
      do you supposes
we can count the poses
      and the ways, fill in the blanks.

The Zaidas kidneys, bladder bursting,
      schlepping tablets, giving thanks,
drinking water, partched and thirsting,
      unloosening girth and tool from loins,
and with an "Oi"
      he did his biz,
that sweet releasing of a whiz,

and then descending,
       words in hand,
to the crazy crowd below,
       to condemn them for their heathen how,
Ye Gods, the worship of a cow!
       Oi, to chuck it all and flee.
But all old Moses did,
       was pee! Another Oi, said he.

Remember Jo'shua who walked the Earth,
       as we are doin.
He had the hydraulic urge too,
       and stopped what he was doing.
Upon the "Mount",
       Jesus held it in.
What were those lapses in the Gospels,
prayers and Holy vows,
       just the slips of someone's pen?

Or take Gautama,
       by the stream;
many long years, he did sat,
       just think of that.

Again, lapses in the teaching,
       to be excused,
dare I say it?
       The Buddha,
when he shat.

So don't it all come down to this:
When Goddess Mother Nature calls,
       Well!

It's time to piss.
Consider this:
      When on Deities you ponder
in your brain,
      It's no wonder,
the deeds they did,
      their holy passion,
their pious flame.

Weren't they just human,
      equipped the same as we?
And GOD is great,
      our devotion, given free,
He imbued us, great and small,
      with the humbling thing,
saints and sinners al,
      just like you and me.
Oh GOD, you must be laughing;
      we're the same,
on this base level;
      One and all,
we have to pee!
      And God forgive my impiety.

      – July 24-25, 1997

Contact

Oh fellow dust mites,
Such fragile: atoms, nuclei therein, protons, electrons, gluons,
       quarks, z particles, ad infinitum.
Oh fragile fleshy things,
Lost, lost in the stars,
Not even a jot in the vast ocean of time or the movement of
       a particle,
Trying to find our celestial course-roots through
       Astrophysics.
Was it the "BIG BANG" or the facile quietude of a
       spontaneous "VACUUM GENESIS"?
Scientists are trying to find the first logic in the first
       partiseconds, to peer into the mind of GOD.
We have become the Reality, wondering what HE has
       wrought.
This lump of clay, this feeble flesh, this odd collection of
       what we are told resembles the universe, down to our
       subatomic structure!
And Steven Hawkings says, "Even if we did find out, it really
       doesn't matter that much."
What really matters is, how do we care for one another in a
       world besieged with all manner of fear and terror,
As we try to solve the mystery of the life of the universe.

              – October 27, 1997

Laura's Manger

Here we are at Laura's place, a gaggle of poets, all asleep,
The day breaking upon us at a beach called Stinson.
An overcast sky outlines a Paynes grey ocean,
Shorebirds frolick along the shoreline before the sunless
dawn,
as Plovers and Seagulls bathe in the frothy surf.
Someone is snoring softly in the background of this multi-
windowed room fronting on the beach,
but not as loud as last night's "K.L." buzz snore.
The morning's background, soft rhythmic snorer, awakens
me at 7,
as the hydraulic urgency propels me towards the head.
Surveying round, I see Vernon slept outside, in his cocooned,
sleeping bag, with a tarp overcovering against the ocean spray.
I retired to the great yellow couch, sheeted and pillowed for,
sleep. Firm enough for my aching back.
As I scribble these lines, Benedictine Monks chant holy
prayers,
in cadenced metre, co-joining feelings of peace and gratitude
to be amongst the living experience of you all.
Memories of different people, places and times come
flooding back.
The ocean surf, nature's perpetual motion-machine, rolls and
breaks, pounding on.
Like the ancient Hebrew Kaddish prayer, described as
"pounding, and soothing" the "pounds and soothes" of
Siegel's poem.
Oh ye sages, were you Angels amongst us, unknowing?
Chansons sing-song in my ears, accompanying such thoughts.
How could we know that the only thing we shall take with us
at the end of our journey would be names and memories?
Thanks the Living GOD, Gods and Goddesses for letting us

dwell amongst sages, poets, friends who care.
Bana's little Shih a Tzu faithfully sleeps beside her,
here in Laura's manger of a house, above the beach,
as the surf continues to roll, break and pound below us,
in this quietude of a reflective, Sunday morn.

– July 26-27, 1997

The Biz

In the latter part of the day,
                     people may buy,
or not buy or pay,
                They want the goods for less,
                               they say.
Italianos
        especially put it this way:
                     Dropo,
                         dropo,
                             dropo da price,
down
     and
         away,
             or we no pay.
                Injuns from India
                        exclaim,
                             Too
                               costly,
too costly,
        the costlies say,
                'tis cheepur,
                     in my country.
The costlies they say,
            I'm not RAJA,
                    I'm poor from Jaipur.
Inscrutable Orientals,
                we surmise have a good stash,
they ask,
        Honorable salesman,
                    how much for cash?
Mr. your price too high, too tight.
So as I try to saff the sale up,

I think to myself,
O.K. and YEAH RIGHT!
All day long,
spaghetti benders,
Deutschers,
and Costlie B.B.'s alike,
ounce for ounce,
try to break balls,
big time,
before they will bounce.
'Tis a poor salesman's lot,
see a sale B.O. and fizzzz,
just a typ-i-cal day
in the Camera Biz.
So upright stand we,
staid of heart,
and,
now for our part,
what can we show, as the Boss checks us out?
He hollers his quiz:
You're kidding OF COURSE!
WHA HAPPEN TO THE BIZ?
And HEY!!
Was anybody working here today????!!!!....

Taqueria

A man disheveled-looking suddenly barges into the lavatory
as I'm whizzing, forcing the catch on the door which I know
I secured as I entered the bathroom. He starts to run hot
water to splash on his face which is cut and bruised and looks
like he was in a fight and got the worst of it. This man
seems to not respect anyone's privacy or rights especially,
now, mine.

      Later sitting down now in my favorites Mission
Salvadoran Taqueria I order my Salvadoran steak dinner.
After ordering, sitting reading some tome, in strides the man
from the bathroom, all six feet two of him. Messily dressed,
he stands before the cashier-waitress and yells "Where's the
fucken money order I gave you last night? I was supposed to
get change from it!!" He stands around for many minutes as
the waitress is busily serving and taking orders from other
diners. He scratches himself like a mongrel, menacingly
demanding the pretty waitress instantly give him what he
wants. She says "Señor, I can do nothing for you now, only
my Boss, who is not here now." He starts bellowing "Get the
owner, the owner, get the owner, NOW!!" As the waitress
brings over my salsa and chips I tell her "He is obviously a
'Mishnoon', a crazy, you can see it in the wild shifting eyes,
you learn this in dealing with people in retail, right away."

      "My money, my money, I want it now!" he screams.
"Sorry, señor, mañana." Suddenly he reaches towards the
kitchen ledge. Sitting there is a large pot of steaming tomato
sauce. He tips it over, it splashing onto the Mexican design
brown rug, tomatoes everywhere, splashing a lady waiting for
a takeout. She screams "I'm burnt", the sauce creating a
Jackson Pollackesque pattern, almost like a mandala.
Suddenly emerging from the kitchen, three stout Salvadoran
cooks, almost lookalikes with their hair done up bun style,

36

squat peasant stock, strong. One is armed with a cat o' nine tails. Striking at him like the front four of a football team they block him towards the door as the one with the nine tails flicks it at him every so often. Out into the cold of Sixteenth Street he is pushed, disappearing as suddenly as he appeared, all of us diners staring towards the door shocked, dumbfounded, immune.

– January 1995

Alta Cocka Transit, Vrrrroom, Vrooom!

By Gad,
the Goddamned bus company
says they'll discontinue service,
only 230 to 250 thousand riders,
first cancel sixteen buses,
then thirty-two, sixty-four, then, then,
raise the fares again!
1:25 to Hearst, 2:50 to Solano, 3:00 to Ashby,
disembowel the runs,
Sorry kids, no more A.C. to school,
Old folks up the hill,
no more sixty-five or sixty-seven down Grizzly,
roll down the damn hill,
Ya'll in Berzerkeley take a forty-three,
the F is gone, gone, gone,
sans Transbay,
Go Bart yourselves,
up the fares.
A.C. your partners in Dis Service,
Recession, squandered funds by former A.C.
board members,
a supervisor couldn't account for ten million,
Hey A.C. rider,
stay home,
watch T.V.,
Bart yourself, body to body,
to pay the rent and fare thee well,
Hell, Hell, Hell,
wherefore are we, tell, tell, tell.....me.

— September 1991

My Father's Face (for Leo Kottke)

all asleep in the same dream,
 Everyone's bed, floor, sidewalk, bush,
   piece of dirt,
    Same dream, same dream,
     You get up and look,
      out the window, the window,
      out the window,
       look, see,
        the Moon, the stars,
         through the window,
          the same dream,
           You look in the mirror,
            See the wan smile of your father,
             your mother,
              as the sun rises, slowly now,
               gaining speed, as the day goes,
                faster now, ever so much,
                 through the window, the window,
                  'Tis but a dream now,
                   the sunset, Mother and Father,
                    going down together, too quick,
                     too quick,
                      Just you now,
                       the Moon, and the stars,
                        going down, down,
                         through the window,
                          the window,
                           and the mirror of your soul..........

For Anda Glass 1960-1987

This is how the very fragile Anda Glass died,
Anda even tho a wheel chair M.S. invalid,
was a poet.
A person with only a twenty-seven year lifespan
on this planet,
Anda laughed when Dan,
her live-in attendant, made jokes.
Scott, her other roommate, couldn't sleep some nights,
when Anda moaned, all night long in her room.
Unbeknownst to Anda, her mother also developed M.S.
Days passed by and Anda began to lose control of
the muscles in her throat, the ones that let her
swallow, But while she could, she wrote:
"A beautiful day is My hearts desire,
to share the brilliance of the day, and laugh with
friends is My hearts desire."
and, "I'm a Daisy in a flower field,
now trying to smile, as My petals are ripped
asunder, by you, from my stem."
Soon Anda's hands wouldn't work,
couldn't inscribe, works her mind would describe.
Eventually her mouth and tongue couldn't
ask for simple requests such as, "I'm hungry"
or "I have to go to the bathroom."
But she wrote in her poetry journal:
"I hate being disabled, I can't glide like
a Swan, I try to look nice, but it doesn't make
any difference, people notice." "I like to
walk in the dark so I won't have to look
at peoples eyes" and
"She could not speak,
She was incapable of the gift,

It was not allowed for her,
for her gift of beauty was to replace her tongue.
She never did shed a tear for the loss
of her speech, for the world would treat her so
unkind,
And now she called forth agonizing sympathy
that was to become her power of destruction
and the peoples unconscious mourning."
The brutality of incontinency made her
feel she wasn't human anymore.
One day she shriveled like a dried prune
that had moaned in agony for years, she
lost the ability to breather and simply
stopped breathing in the hospital.
Dan and Scott after their mourning had
her cremated.
Now in a small brass cubed box, on the shelf,
alongside the thirty-one volumes of the
Encyclopedia Britannica, under the white lamp
in our house, are the fragments of the once
very beautiful, Anda Glass.

— January 1987

Pegasus

I continue the odyssey as I fly through my personal gauntlet now, the Southwest Airlines 737 air shuttle back and forth for medical exigencies. Little did I ever consider that I'd be in such a situation. However this brief flight flying above the dense cloud cover before dawn, this svelte craft piercing the dark clouds revealing the dark beauty of its airscape tundra rolling to the horizon. This ship carrying one hundred thirty five lives within its streamlined interior hull, like the womb carrying the child. No wonder that ships and planes are referred to as "SHE". She's a var good ship, Matey.

We steeply climb and level out at thirty-five thousand feet and level off, our ship shuddering ever so the wings vibrating sensing the heavier cloudy air streamlining contrails receding behind the wing tips. The oceans of cumulous dark, rolling majestically, gently moving. Within the interior its immenseness containing millions of gallons of moisture, potentially enormous downpours of rain, snow, sleet, hail, when conditions ripen it will be vented on terra firma.

Flying releases such strange thoughts considering the tenuous problem passengers always must feel. But our ship's Captain and crew are a bonnie bunch steering an even keel. I recall the wonderful descriptions of the majesty and skill of flying in the descriptions by the immortal Antoine de Saint-Exupéry, the great French poet and military pilot, author of *The Little Prince*. But his real prose comes alive when he writes about his experiences of flight. The mail routes in rickety single prop or bi-planes flying the mail routes or over battlefields during the Spanish war with his comrades but sitting mostly the lone eagle. Flying amongst the clouds, wind, sand, stars, sitting in an uncanopied cockpit the conditions obscuring the reading of instrumentation flying by instinct alone. The lone pilot and the elements.

As I glance out the porthole hints of sunstreaks begin
to illuminate the dark mass of clouds some miles distant; the
heavy cloud cover begins to respond to the light and heat of
the sun millions of miles away in our galaxy as the planet
revolves to catch its life force. The bloody orb rises slowly
above the cloud canopy, boiling, piercing, pushing above the
dark, bursting forth in a volcano of brilliance. The
devastating glare overwhelming the landscape. Transforming
the hanging dark clouds into beautiful billows of fluffy white
cotton.

Saint-Exupéry's descriptions of flying over Spain
during its Fascist war are very compelling. Observing the
pathetic battles below, he writes, "Faintly visible was
something that I guessed to be smoke. Was that one of the
signs that I was seeking? Was this a scrap of evidence of that
nearly soundless anger whose all-destroying wrath was so
hard to measure? A whole civilization was contained in that
faint golden puff so lightly dispersed by a breath of wind."
And elsewhere in his writing , observing little white puffs
again on a battlefield, Antoine realizes that it is the remnants
of gas ejection from the rifles and men are at the ultimate
folly of warfare and trying to kill one other.

And it still continues in this so-called modern age
careening towards the Millennium. Somewhere on the other
side of our planet I am sad to report it's Yugoslavia's turn to
suffer. Killing them pell-mell in a high tech terrifying way.
The crafts of death and destruction rain down on killers and
innocents simultaneously. On this beautiful globe, with all
its natural beauty and majesty, the devastation continues.

But consider. I consider. My oncologist in Southern
California is a lovely Vietnamese woman of considerable
brilliance and competence, and most of all compassion.
Another in Adventura, Florida, a Palestinian oncologist, is

also brilliant and competent, is a professor of medicine and cancer researcher of great import. Her name is Dr. Bicklin Nyugen. His is Dr. Artef Hussein. These two have either gone through or heard firsthand about the terrible recent reigns of terror, suffering the painful horrors of war and its pestillance, and yet here they are fighting for people's lives, strangers they have never met, with great compassion yet.

How many holocausts shall continue to plague our planet? Isn't it enough that these terrible plagues continue also? How many individuals of great courage and brilliance have been killed? How many are being eradicated from within our multitude and are being lost? And I know I am raking up old concerns. But it must be disseminated to new generations in a cogent way.

PLEASE DO NOT TRIVIALIZE THIS WITH A BORED "I KNOW" PLATITUDE. How many generations shall commit murder on another again and again? Thou shall not kill has become a morally inane senseless commandment in a society that worships death. The name of GOD is intoned over and over again. Parroted as a caveat to committing murder.

Here in a society that has a death wish advertizing wholesale in motion pictures on T.V. and in the literature, we have become jaded and immune to murder. The slaughterhouse is open for business twenty-four hours a day. On the streets and on the battlefields, in our homes and schools, we feed it to our babies with their milk and cookies, and almost in the womb. Isn't it enough the things that will kill us accidentally or from diseases? We'll rake up all the old religious jihads of vengeance to wreak all manner of torture and death on one another. Sometimes for nothing at all? Just a form of Vampirism which is trivialized and becomes a cult of insanity. Murder that individual of different skin color or other persuasion or speech and that different way of worshiping GOD. How utterly insane. Murder, subdue, disenfranchise the have-nots for the territorial imperative or the greed of power and capital, continuing the long long generations of Biblical evolutionary Darwinistic hatreds. We are losing people who may discover cures for the incurable, politicians skilled in transforming war into peace and compassion. Heal the old wounds. As long as the accumulation of wealth and power continue the road of greed we shall suffer over and over again. The message of Christ and Buddha, Mohammed is revolutionary of course. People FIRST! Where is that utopian wished-for Shangri-la where we all live in a fearless tranquility? The fairy tale, Live long and prosper?

The choice is frighteningly upon us to stop the madness, stop the killing, stop the killing or choose death, be slaughtered in wholesale nuclear genocide, give in to the Biblical wished-for prophecy.

Is this what we really want?
Or shall we give our babies a terror-free sane compassionate future?

We must choose LIFE.
— April 12, 1999

Flights of Compassion

For the first time in my life I am being humbled, by a disease,
Taken down at the knees like a martial arts master,
Reduced to begging to get on an airplane
once every two weeks to travel,
Five hundred miles to dove tail,
for a chance that the oncological elixir will help
prolong my life.
But it is such a difficult task master,
Navigating the intricacies of the enigma of arrival,
and affordability of traveling,
Ironically reduced to the status
of begging strangers to help get you there on time.
They imply of my ingratitude of receiving
two previous complimentary flights,
But ladies I am not ungrateful,
I am fighting now to take advantage of low priced fares.
I am told regretfully that they have been sold out in advance,
Other more savvy frequent fliers have purchased them way in
        advance,
only so many people fit onto those 737's.
I realize I am caught in the corporate trap, inadvertently,
Their consternation to help evident when they try to explain
the failure of a system so ponderous as its people struggle,
trying to help,
And I hear it in their voices and it echoes in mine.
The ladies are trying to make me understand through my
own frustrations, they are Angels, listening to my pleading,
As I cry out, they say, "I understand, but..."
My reply the thinking no one understands unless you're
fighting for your LIFE! That no one can help you, because,
it is not in my vocabulary,
And the situation, running dialogue has a life of its own

deafness, as it brings me to my knees again, with the phrase,
I am just one of thousands of similar cases that have had to
be turned away, what a thing to say, a karate chop to the ego,
They understand but cannot help, implied is I may have to
pay that which I simply cannot afford,
The ironic reality of situation.
Know that this thing can wipe you out in every way
emotionally, spiritually, and now logistically, financially,
But I won't let it, the old Wu Li master in me takes a stance,
All of my instincts of many years like YODA, I feel the force
And I begin to fight the war of words, parrying, thrust, feign,
With my twenty-seven little soldiers flowing through mind
and tongue, I become the perfectly imperfect master,
With my words and training, but words only,
I firmly but gently force them to find a way for me,
with the Tao of my language, emotion which is true,
And gratefully I bow and beg forgiveness humbly,
And am grateful to all and GOD for the way to
                    compassionate flight.

                    – April 12, 1999

Mr Fukin El Niño to You

Hey yo, Compadre! muchacho sheet-head,
 This is El Niño,
  And I'm comin to kick yo little tukas.
  Hey! Yo Califor-nio!!
   Gonna blow you down, down, down.
    I'll huff, and I'll puff,
     Yeah! Gonna kick me some West Coast ass!
     Don't give me none of that, what chu mean, shit!
     Gonna piss on yo pro-per-ty, for a l-o-n-g time,
       Mu-tha Fu-ka!
       Hey, yo, Comprende Vu?
       Yo Su-kka! Better vamoose, pequeño Goose,
       Cause I'm a bad Mutha-Fukka,
        And I'm looking for you!
         Gonna thirty-foot wave your shores,
          Gonna blow all them trees down!
           Gonna sling my mud at chu
           and throw some sheeyat!
           Gonna overflow
            all your rivers, streams, lakes, creeks,
           Gonna throw you out! Sukka!
            Sat-ur-ate, agi-tate, til you say, unc-le!
             What chu say? Yeah, I may give you a day off,
             But tom-orr-ow, I'll be back!
                To kick Yo-Ass again and break your balls.
What chu say? Who sent me? Hey, Yo! Momma Nay-ture.
                                          that's who,
     And it's, MR. EL NIÑO, to you,
        Mu-tha Fuk-ka,
          And don't you for-get it eitha, Suk-ka!

48

After Days of 1988 (after Cavafy)

I.   He was the bright new "Bunny Boy"
of Castro Street.
      A young forty-nine year old
slim, finely muscled, bearded Australian,
British satyr.
      An erotic tendency to flirt
and be flirted with.
      Walking alongside his new ten-speed,
as sleek and finely tuned.
      Outfitted in the latest latex
racing fashions....
      Ignoring the warnings,
thinking he was immune to the Angel of Death.
      "Should you be seen with him,
your reputation surely would be compromised."
      Explaining this all away as a
reliving of his teenage, pubescent years
claiming he'd lost, with the bird of his youth.

II.   His favorites were tall girlish
Malaysians, lured with his collection
of pornographic magazines, glistening
with penises like banana stalks.

        Kept and supported by older
vain, bearded men
        With more or less freedom of movement,
complaining of sexual slavery.
        Unmonogamous, untrustworthy,
pilferer of feelings and things.
        A child in the sexual candy store
that was San Francisco of the Mid-Eighties
        Renamed by his straight friend "D"
San Fran-Crisco Californica to his delite.
        At spare off moments
while his older lovers were off, working,
unaware that he was selling "alley B.J.'s"
buying a tryst, in a lavatory or
clandestinely in his boudoir.

III.   "D" wondered to himself
How compromised was he?
A medical history of dangerously
low blood pressure,
many days slept away,
a daily diet of Godsend prednisone,
cortisone bone destroyer,
trying to regain his composure.
          Leading a double charmed
underground life.
          Ingratiating himself into your
life with a charmed ease, reeking of
literacy and to whit, seducing all
within his province, with a high British
accent, gleaned from a tutelage in
New Zealand's finest Christ Church
prep schools.
          Disdained offspring of a peerage Australian
family, disowned by an angry brother.
          Cuddled by a remarried mother,
bankrolled by his titled peerage stepmom.

IV.   Penchants shocking and hidden.
His secret life, known only to confidants.
Australian surf bum, luxurious life physical,
seductive, muscularity ravaging all totally
within his province.

His fait accompli
a wished-for, self-fulfilled, early demise.
Uncaring attitudes, resigning all
us to suffer his early, Earthly absence.

Essence so intertwinedly of
so many lives, his love burning
in our hearts forever.

Touched by his passion,
fire, brilliance.

This world someday
takes us all away, Artists, Scientists, Poets,
et al.

Disrespectful Dolts,
unheeding life's warnings,
passion, sweeping all away to recklessness,
there is no immortality in youth or beauty.

All is vanity.

Sun and Moon

The Dalai Lama
looks for the child
Panchen Lama.

As the Sun looks
for the Moon,
the Moon awaits
the Sun of the Dalai Lama.

For each divine lifetime,
one waits for the other,
this evolving cyclical
thing of Divinity,
happening on the
rotating, blue-green,
watery, earthen marble, hurtling through space and time,
so fragile, as to implode,
or explode and cease to
be at any moment,
along with us fleshy
things, borne from the
earth elements,
life breathed into us,
to hope for the 7th
cycle of K,
where we have been
to Hell and back
many times,
the Dalai Lama instructing
the other lamas, who shall tell us
finally when we
get it right.

Jazz Fusion Universe

It all starts with the scratch of carbon,
on paper.
Tools of the despised material workers,
as W.C.W. once put it.
This Handmaiden of the cerebral cortex
suffuses the Jazz in my mind with
radio talk describing a self-replicating
molecular based machine,
future where our sentient society
may transcend to one of pure thought,
and spirit, an auto-cloning world,
directing its own Frankenstein,
doing its bidding at a whim,

              or

We're free to contemplate
      a lavender sun's setting fire
            Jimmy Smith's
                  cascading organ blues
His riffs sending us
            Into our own inner, outer space
                  And
the blue twinkle
            or sapphire fire
In a loved one's eye
                  or
This drug-free endless high
in the Elysian Universe

As
Coltrane and Bird
Bring us back to Ellingtonia
the sheer musical
pleasure
of this jazz fusion
Universe,
shifting
and
changing,
Like
Brubeck,
to
Desmond,
to Morello,
Can you dig my meaning, Man?
going higher and higher
the sounds the high
man, the sounds the high,
Life's own musik
Mein Herr.

Speak Memory

To freeze the moment, to seize it, make it last, make it last,
That clutch of body to body,
Feeling the curve of a breast, its sweet sensuous weight,
Cupped in palm, that light, heaviness of fleshly fat,
Saltiness of nipple in mouth to tongue,
The fuck,
And permeating smell of sex, the after ecstasy of fucking,
as it perfumes the air,
Flesh on flesh passion, especially for someone you love,
Butt to butt, eating at the Y, laughing,
That moment of defenselessness, a sweet letting go,
The clench, the swoon, the sigh from a high,
a touch of inner thigh, breasts on eyelids,
A special sensory feel, smiling, almost indescribable,
Of memory only, changing with time, eyes closed,
Called forth from memory only, speak memory,
Fading, fading, words, words, words only,
$$\text{to remember}$$

$$- \text{April 4, 1998}$$

Written in the Belly of the Beast

It is five-thirty of a Friday morning as I awaken to the mournful sound of the Southern Pacific freight train's passage alongside Berkeley California's perimeter.

    Its train whistle reverberating to my nostalgic consciousness reminds me of other times and places that I've lived. In the northeast Hudson Valley at Ossining, New York. That corridor riding and listening to its freights and passenger commuter trains' whistles rites of passage only a few thousand feet from the house I shared with my ex-wife alongside the idyllic riverside.

    Or remembering her own house in Winston-Salem, N.C. where during our courtship a nearby mournful whistle echoed calling to something deep in me. Remember these times in your life it seemed to say, I think now. Mark this!

    And I remember the simple railroad apartment I grew up in, in the mid-Bronx. Never having my own room. I in my infant's railed bed, in my parents' bedroom heard even then the whistle calling from a few blocks away as a freight ran alongside the Bronx River, with its cement factories and fishing boats that would party boat fishermen out to the then clean Long Island Sound for a day's catch. Growing up here the whistle sounded, Mark this! The bittersweet years of my youth.

    The whistle called as I sped away to an airport in New Jersey leaving my "Ex" back at the riverside house for San Francisco. Hoping to re-start my life again. Mark this!

    Beginning my odyssey in this final "Enigma of Arrival" here on the West Coast. Setting down my roots again to connect. With all that that entailed. The constant relocating to find a perch to land. The struggle to find employment and friends. Rediscovering, reinventing myself, acclimating to this new old vital place.

Becoming the writer I wanted to be engaging the community of new contemporary poets of San Francisco and Berkeley that I joined and love.

Letting it all hang out, I opened my heart again to Love. Suffering through three "Her-A-Cained" affairs, leaving me like those tornadoed Midwest towns, totally ripped asunder. Vulnerable to their vicissitudes leaving my body emotionally and physically vulnerable to all the "ills that flesh is heir to". A town without pity.

So here I am battling a dreaded life-threatening disease, where your own body turns against you. Nature is trying to send me a message and I am trying to get it. As I struggle to comprehend the spiritual and scientific path of surviving, beseeching my doctors for help. The poor oncologists' sense of failure with all the technology burning them out in the struggle. As I go for the newest hoped-for chemological "CrapShoot", that this investigational protocol will buy me some more time or conquer the invader, while it kicks my butt with its chemological peccadillos, or side effects.

At this writing I await the latest in Cat-Scans this coming Monday, having done twenty-five pounds of them already, my co-pay at $310.00 each. This all to see whether flying four round trips by plane every two weeks from Berkeley to Fountain Valley Hospital was worth it. This demanding heavy-duty protocol entailing ninety-six hours of continuing chemo over a three-day period which ends at my clinic at Berkeley. When I return to some sense of relief for two weeks, vacationing at my part-time job.

However the last three days have been quite an ordeal caught up in the onslaught of both clinics besieged to the rafters with cancer patients needing relief from the plague. As the nurses vainly struggle I suffer delay of treatment, which becomes a mini-crisis for me ending up

58

spending more than the ninety-six dreaded hours. One of the hundred or more people in crisis. Refugees from a cruel overbearing enemy trying to holocaust us. With precious little to save the life leaking away from us. The technology in pursuit of cure successful if caught early enough but not so easy when you're "Stage 4" and it has spread. So I'm hoping to catch the "Brass Ring" of remission but it's only a 25% chance as Dr. Cohen and Dr. Nguyen put it.

So I hope against hope, praying to GOD and HIS ANGELS every day, my life becoming a constant prayer in all my thoughts, as my reality becomes ever so palpable, reverbing within my consciousness, its whistle blows now and then. I am writing from the heart and soul, mindfully. My experience, personal and impersonal at once, but from this individual's consciousness, nay experience. I give voice to this honestly as I write and say my prose and poetry if you will. A life in prose, a speaking poem wrought in these twenty-seven little soldiers that shall speak for me when I can't.

So I'm in the clinic the life-saving pump and my body not cooperating to absorb the chemo into my veins. And the pump's little micro-computer won't budge as the RN's are at their wits' end to help me. And a sense of panic is afoot as I sense that an inordinately long amount of time is passing as they page for help. I alight from the bed in the little cubicle they'd been working with me in. I go to the frontage area where they are convening. The look of concern for their ignorance on how to proceed without doing more damage to me. I suggest the special pharmacy in Berkeley where a special Infusion Pharmacist is on duty until 8 P.M. to advise in such a crisis. Meanwhile they have paged a special charge nurse who is also very knowledgeable. Both calls return simultaneously and I am rescued to continue the demanding protocol which will mercifully end today at three. (It is now 10:50 A.M., Friday, as my pump continues to

chemocize, infusing through my veins as I write this. Come 6
P.M. or sooner, I hope it shall release me from my bondage.)

I prayed to my GOD, and all the other Deities, to
see me through this long ordeal. I the human needle-pin-
cushion. Stabbed four times in the chest, now it seems for
lack of foresight and analyzing the situation mindfully.

I pray to TARA, nurse of the world, as my
meditation becomes a tool of overcoming my fear and sense
of panic. I am ever so grateful for learning how to do this, it
allows me to laugh at my fears and distract my mind. As an
illustration I think of the absurd depiction played by Bill
Murray, as a crazy masochist. Playing against his character is
the other comedian, Steve Martin, playing a deranged Dentist
in the movie of the play *Little Shop of Horrors*, and I laugh
to myself.

As the bizarre side effects turn you into a
chemological marionette. You have to traverse a diabolical
"Wonderland". But if you ask and read the research you can
steel yourself to get through it.

I have learned to become my own Oncologist, Nurse,
Researcher, Deficit Financial Counselor, Social Security,
Social Worker, Patient Advocate, Administrative Counselor,
and General People Counsel to become the interactive glue
between everyone that can help. You must sew together an
elaborate support system. If you work it's with your Boss
and fellow employees, if possible your family (so important!),
and with all the above, my fellow poets, my readers (the few),
all my friends, bless them all, new friends, strangers I've just
met or will meet.

To discover the world anew asking for help in a
respectful friendly way, controlling your fears and panic. I
believe in the ultimate goodness of people. With all the
terrible current events of a world in trouble, still love is the
answer, but it is a world of learning to make it work. To

bring the spirit of the true GOD of mercy and kindness into your heart you must learn to be the spirit of Compassion so that GOD and HIS ANGELS are residing within. I put this all down with respect and love for you all. Myself and the WORLD. Thanking all of my venerable teachers, I let this all go and pass it on. I am open for more teaching and instruction. I hope to make a contribution, to share some of what I have learned by helping to create a web site with the help of people and to make it a permanent help line for people like myself who didn't have a clue on how to find "The Way" to negotiate the complicated path to remote chemological protocols. All the social workers say this is sorely needed, but to make it work eventually everyone's own experieince and knowledge shall be needed. I envision a full-time proposal shall be ultimately necessary.

A holy man I have never met, this is his holy vision. I should like to pass it on to the reader.

With Love,

Richard N. "Dixi" Cohn
May 7, 1999

One day some people came to the master and asked:
How can you be happy in a World of such impermanence?
Where you cannot protect your loved ones from
harm, illness and death?
The Master held up a glass and said:
Someone gave me this glass, and I really like this glass.
It holds my water admirably. I touch it and it rings!
One day the wind may blow it off the shelf, or my elbow
may knock it from the table. I KNOW THIS GLASS IS
ALREADY BROKEN SO I ENJOY IT INCREDIBLY.
(the Venerable Achaan Chan Subato)

Sixty-Six Buses or Lost on Muni

I looked for You,
   riding *Muni,*
      night and day,
Rode with *Geary,* all the way.
Corbett told me
    I'd find you at *O'shaunessy's,*
But ride, ride on,
    I did, on a *Three Day Passport,*
Looking, looking for you,
      through Babylon by the Bay,
Up and down *Taravel,*
     even *Sunday Taravel,*
I got an *Ocean View,*
    but no you,
Ride on, *Judah* said,
   and *Teresita*
      gave me a clue,
Possibly at *Ingleside,*
    there'd be a *Church,*
and you'd be inducted into *Masonic* rides,
along with *Bryant* and *Hayes.*

The first night of the first day,
    looking, looking,
for you,
  The *Owl* told me about the *Sunset,*
and *Stanyan Sunday,*
    He'd seen you while flying,
over *Eureka,*
   Eureka! Sunday!

But I still hadn't found the *Gateway*,
Balboa and *Clement* said I was an *Excelsior* individual,
But *Felton* told me to look for you in *Rutland*,
where they spoke *Quintana*,

                        I said I *Haight* it there,
almost as much as *Noriega*,

                        I wouldn't drive my
Laguna Honda there,

                    I'd rather do *Divisidero* at *Folsom*,
than break our *Union*,

                    t'would be as bad as
Coit us interruptus, in *Valencia*.
You drove me to *Bernal Heights*,
and showed me the *Pacific* once,
Together in *Southern Heights*,

                        we shared a
Golden Gate.

                Were *Parnassas* in *California*,
Could he be *Fillmore?*

                    On my *Mission* to the *Market*
I consulted *Powell*, *Mason* and *Hyde*.
That led me to *Jackson* in *San Bruno*.
By the *Ferry* at the *Marina*,

                    Levi said you got off
the *Cal Train*

                  at *Van Ness* and fell asleep on the
Downtown Loop.

                  You told me you forgot where you
*Park*ed the *Merced*,

                probably in the *Marin Headlands*,

As I kissed you,
          The *Red and White, Blue and Gold*
Sunset in *Sam Trans,*
               And *A.C.* was happy in the East Bay,
You said you were *Fulton* with me in *Stockton,*
But we both know that the bus to *Paradise*
doesn't stop here, anymore.

— April 1991